EFFECT...
OF T...

CW00595019

by Roy Pernet

with an additional chapter by David Wright

The Industrial Society

First published 1979 by
The Industrial Society
Robert Hyde House
48 Bryanston Square
London W1H 7LN
Telephone: 071 – 262 2401

Second edition 1989
© The Industrial Society, 1979, 1989
Reprinted 1990, 1991, 1992

ISBN 0 85290 429 0

British Library Cataloguing in Publication Data
Pernet, Roy
    Effective use of time.—2nd ed.
    1. Organisations. Managers. Time. Allocation,—Manuals
    I. Title II. Industrial Society III. Series
    658.4'093

Typeset by Columns Ltd, Reading
Printed and bound in Great Britain by Belmont Press, Northampton

CONTENTS

FOREWORD

Whatever the discipline or level of management, the responsibilities of a manager are many and various. It is their job to produce results with essentially just two resources—people and time.

To maximise the potential of both, most managers need some reminders and basic guidelines to help them.

The Notes for Managers series provides succinct yet comprehensive coverage of key management issues and skills. The short time it takes to read each title will pay dividends in terms of utilising one of those key resources—people.

ALISTAIR GRAHAM
Director, The Industrial Society

INTRODUCTION

These notes have been put together to help the busy manager get on top of some ever-present problems, such as:

- backlog of paperwork
- continual interruptions
- domination by the telephone
- instant reactions to urgent problems (regardless of their relative importance)
- falling asleep (on the train or at home) trying to catch up on some reading.

Lack of time is often used as a cover for inefficiency, lack of forethought, delays, or failures. It is no use muttering about 'theory' or 'an ideal world'. In reality we *have* to get things done in a far from perfect setting. Proper management of time is crucial to the success of organisations. Yet so much is left to chance.

- Where do the best ideas come from?
- How are decisions made?
- Do we use basic, taken for granted skills (like reading and writing) properly?
- Are our meetings short and productive, and do things get done on schedule?

I

EFFECTIVE USE
OF TIME

1

THINKING

There is a strong belief that we have to look busy all the time—or at least when the boss can see us. The idea of taking time off to stop and think produces uneasy feelings. Yet thinking must be a central part of productive work. To do it properly calls for concentration, self-discipline and proper allocation of time for the purpose.

Example 1
A senior official in a professional institute advises members to spend a period of every day in thought. He tries between 3 p.m. and 5 p.m. What about? About what exactly he is paid to achieve, and how his group can make a better contribution.

Example 2
The London manager of an international concern periodically climbs into a 'mental helicopter' and views the topic under discussion from a vantage point up in the ceiling. Her colleagues have grown used to her occasional trances.

Not all thinking is directed at solving work problems. The brain needs frequent short concentration breaks, and we can use some of the day's interruptions in this way. Neither does the mind switch off when we have found a solution. We can get much pleasure from spontaneous mental freewheeling and unwinding.

Example 3
A construction engineer asserts that, when he breaks away from 'banging my head against a brick wall', he experiences two remarkable effects: 'The pain goes, and my vision clears.'

3

So, not only should we set aside some time for serious work-thinking, but we should also tolerate, even welcome, play-thinking. The value of timely thinking cannot be overstressed.

The human brain

Our brains are much more efficient than we give ourselves credit. We now know that the brain has a much greater ability than was previously believed. Tiny babies have an enormous capacity to learn and develop; far from being 'helpless little things' they grow intellectually at a pace far outstripping current advances in computer technology.

The athlete knows the value of regular training for the next race. The executive with middle-age spread will admit the possibility of getting back into trim with appropriate visits to the local sports centre (not forgetting changes in diet). The brain, too, needs regular exercise to attain a high level of efficiency.

We can think a lot faster than we can talk. The average person can speak at about 200 words per minute. Tests show we can habitually think at over 600 wpm. Perhaps this suggests we can gain an advantage by more listening and less interrupting. We could use the extra seconds gained, deciding from a range of possible replies, instead of relying on instinct.

It pays to listen properly. School leavers at work, who found it hard to respect their supervisors, levelled one criticism most often: 'They don't listen.'

Creative thinking

We habitually tend to think 'analytically', where logical deduction from known facts leads to a more or less indisputable answer. Most of us are good at this; it is the way we were taught. There are times, however, when we need 'creative' thinking, where imagination is brought into play because the facts do not permit logical deduction.

Creative thinking needs adjusting to. We hit barriers when we first try it. Self-imposed limits to new ideas get in the way: a belief that there is always one right answer; conformity, lack of effort in challenging the obvious; fear of looking foolish. 'That won't work,' we say, and another excellent idea has got away. Creative thinking relates things or ideas not previously related. It can be fun, too. Thoughts proceed in one plane then suddenly veer off in a new direction. The resulting release of tension often leads to laughter. Joke writers know something about this phenomenon.

A successful business thrives on creative thinking. It can stay ahead of the competition with better marketing, improved products and services, and higher motivation. A well-known pen manufacturer improved their performance once someone realised they were in the gift business: the market place took on a new size and shape.

Brainstorming

Brainstorming employs creative thinking to produce lots of ideas quickly. To get the best results, call together a small group of amenable people for about half an hour. Someone has to be able to write the ideas down very quickly—and legibly. Pose the question and encourage a flood of ideas. Once the stream dries up, stop and gaze silently at the chart(s). Allow the ideas to 'incubate' until someone begins to see the 'last piece of the jigsaw'. This is known as the 'AHA!' moment. Sometimes you can look at the silliest idea, pull it apart, and discover yet another usable idea.

The keys to successful brainstorming are:

- getting the problem right; the statement of the question
- consciously and deliberately separating the production of ideas from their evaluation
- letting people whose temperament or mood do not fit the occasion slip away without loss of face.

For private thinking, there is no need for a separate office or a stonewalling secretary for protection. Many people simply avert their gaze from approaching visitors, put up a hand, or turn away for a moment. A good train of thought is hard to get back once interrupted. People respect our need for five seconds' grace.

Lastly, a word about trying too hard to remember little things. The extra effort seems to lock just the word we want on to the tip of our tongue. It can be very embarrassing to forget the boss's name just at the moment of introducing an important visitor. The infuriating fact that the answer pops up — unannounced and unwanted — at a future moment, gives us a clue to how to cope. Don't strain the brain.

2

TIME UTILISATION

If we fail to plan, we plan to fail. Lack of time can become a very emotive issue to many people. Do we really know how we spend it?

In preparing to use our time more effectively, the first things we really need to know are the facts, not the feelings. A record of where our time is really spent is an important first step. There are a number of ways to investigate time utilisation: pre-prepared forms are useful as only 'ticks' or brief notes are necessary. Obviously, this takes a little time, but you can't save time by not spending it. The simplest and most commonly used method is a daily time log (*see* Table 1). Keeping this for a week is probably the best idea.

Other methods for investigating time utilisation are the content of work analysis (*see* Table 2), contacts analysis (*see* Table 3), work priorities diary (*see* Table 4) or the analysis of fleeting contacts (*see* Table 5). In all cases, the headings and layout may be changed to suit individual circumstances.

After analysing the facts that emerge from the investigation, one can then start identifying the real priorities for personal action. One action may be to discuss your time problems and solutions with your boss. Most bosses are much more likely to listen if you have done your homework and come up with suggestions.

Table 1. Daily time log showing major areas of time used

Page . . . . . . Day . . . . . . Date . . . . . .

Day total . . . . . . hrs . . . . . . mins

Summarise weekly for overall picture

Start time	Finish time	Activity	Category of Activity							
		Hrs								
		Mins								

Table 2. Content of work analysis, indicating what you are involved in and who involved you

Brief description of subject	How was I involved? By whom?							Did I need to be concerned?		
	Self	Boss	Subordinate/s	Colleagues	Customers	Others		At all?	At what stage?	In so much detail?

Table 3. Contacts analysis

Length of time	Persons contacted	Brief description of topic

Table 4. Work priorities diary

Time	Brief description of activity	Should I have been doing it then?		Reason for stopping			
		A	B	A	B	C	D
		Yes	No	Finished	Unfinished but necessary	Unnecessary	
						Caused by others	Caused by self

N.B. A tick in columns 3B and/or 4D indicates lack of self-planning

Table 5. Analysis of fleeting contacts

Type of contact		Who was it with?	Who initiated it?		Was it an interruption?
A	B		A	B	
Personal	Phone		Self	Others	

3

DECISIONS

Life is full of decisions. Some are momentous; some are very minor; most are important.

> **Example 4**
> One despairing warehouse superintendent complained that most of his decisions flowed down from an insensitive manager, or 'made themselves' by the pressure of events as the lorries came and went and the forklift trucks went up, down and along. Customers were infuriated with discrepancies. On investigation, it was difficult to find anyone doing anything really wrong. The men were taking short cuts, and some had got into bad habits, learned from their mates.

It is helpful to go to the trouble of *writing down* what it is we are trying to achieve: a statement of the problem. We rarely do this because we assume we know what is wanted. But once we get into the habit of isolating these things on paper, we stand to benefit from the powerful effect it has in sharpening our awareness and clarifying our thoughts. Often, what looks like the central problem turns out to be merely a symptom of something else. Once we are satisfied we have got the problem right, and when we have defined our objective, we are ready for some concentrated thinking. At this stage we generate several possible solutions and try to predict the probable outcome of each.

Now comes the time to decide and act. Choose and implement the most appropriate plan. Communicate it (share, rather than merely transmit). Check at regular intervals to see that the plan is working in practice, or whether it is necessary to re-plan or reorganise. Answer the question: 'Did the action achieve the objective?'

Consider, consult, commit, communicate, check.

4

READING AND WRITING

Time can be irretrievably lost by inefficient use of the skills we were taught when we were very young.

We can measure and perhaps improve on our reading speed (and retention) by working actively through *Rapid reading*.[1] A first step might be simply to read less. Do we have to read every page of every document that comes our way?

We can do a lot about report writing and letter writing. Before diving into the body of the text, think (about the purpose, the readers, the action you want to result). As you write, remember the old 'ABC rule' (accuracy, brevity, clarity). When it's first typed, remember read, check, edit, polish. Good advice is to be found in *Report writing*.[2]

5

TELECOMMUNICATIONS

The telephone

It rings.
'Mr Jones's office.'
'Can I speak to him please?'
'I'm afraid he's not in.'
'Do you know when he'll be back?'
'No, I'm awfully sorry, I don't. Can I take a message?'
'Ah—no, it's all right. I'll ring again later on.'

What has been achieved? Nothing. A recent survey produced the depressing result that 60 per cent of telephone calls failed to produce the information required on the first attempt. Also, less than one person in 10 actually rang back after promising to do so.

With proper training and good leadership, a secretary can choose to handle such a call quite differently.

'Production: Lyn Taylor.' (The voice ends on an upward note.)
'Ah, Ferris here. Bradley and Stokes. Is Frank Jones in?'
'I am expecting him back between 3 and 3.30 this afternoon. Is it something I can help with, Mr Ferris?'
'Well yes, I'm sure you could . . .'

By using our own name in this way, we encourage callers to give their names, too. This saves the awkward 'who's calling?' especially if the party on the other end thinks we ought to recognise the voice. Now that we know who's on the other end, we can decide how much to divulge. We can give the 'bad news' in a positive way. We have organised a time band during which Mr Jones will be available to take and make phone calls. And, as 'god' is away, the caller might just as well parley with one of the angels.

Giving people every chance to work independently (rather than in someone else's shadow) is good: it saves time, and people like to be autonomous.

Example 5

One national public utility is giving its staff special training in answering customers' telephone calls. This idea is to deal completely with the enquiry even when it's not 'our department'. Staff listen carefully, write down the question, read it back and promise action within a specified deadline. Once the call is completed they can discover who the 'right department' is and pass it on with due urgency. No more transferring from one to another—less annoyance, better service, time saved.

Telephone operators have an unusual job which ought to be sympathetically understood by all extension users. The pressures vary between doing nothing and being rushed off one's feet. Everyone can help by spending a moment thinking about what life is like at the console.

Telephone call checklist

1 Decide who to contact, and think of an alternative if they are out.
2 Have a number, dialling code, extension/department written out in front of you.
3 Make brief notes of what is to be told or asked for.
4 Get together any papers you may need to refer to.
5 Make the call. Never let the ringing tone sound more than five times.
6 On reaching the person you want:
   • state who is calling
   • clarify the general purpose of the call

- give the message or ask the question, and check understanding.
7 If you cannot get an answer at once, do not hold on. Offer to ring back after an agreed interval.
8 Ring back when you said you would.

Such a drill has helped to halve the cost of long distance calls, not least by cutting out long and expensive silences. When tariffs are lower in the afternoons, steer clear of the telephone during the mornings.

Computers

Computers will continue to play an increasing role in passing messages of all sorts. Do keep abreast of developments: encourage replacement of old with new devices. Try to introduce systems and procedures which fit national and international agreements—to save time (and money) later.

6

PAPERWORK

The best advice is to get rid of the stuff as soon as you can.

Example 6

The legal adviser in a transport company claims, with a straight face, that she had a drawer in her desk labelled TDTDWT ('too difficult to deal with today').

A busy department head in a registered charity has a tray called GROAN meaning, 'get rid of, anywhere, now!'.

Another manager keeps a big 'OBE' file where he collects things he knows will be overtaken by events.

We may come to resent the onslaught of paper, but to the sender, each bit is an effort to communicate with us. Fewer people than we regularly curse actually set out to annoy. And those who are generating excessive paperwork to justify their existence are only crying out to be loved a little. One good question is, why do *I* have to deal with it all? (*see* Chapter 8).

One way of tackling the job is to put each bit into one of three categories.

1 *Immediate action can be taken*. Do what is called for, make a note in the margin. Into the 'out tray' with it.

2 *Action can be started but not completed*. Do what you can, make a note in the margin. Place in the 'brought-forward' file.[3]

3 *Items for information, reading, circulation*. If it is short you can read it quickly. The more heavy items can be

gathered together and gone through at a planned 'reading time' each day. Do not sit on a circulation item: if you cannot finish it and pass it on within 24 hours make a note for it to be sent back to you when the others on the list have seen it. If you don't need to keep the item, throw it away.

Many replies to internal staff can be handwritten on the incoming memo. Get a photocopy made if you need to keep a record (compare this cost, in time as well as money, with dictation, typing, checking, signing and sending back a formal reply). Have a supply of little memos run off on the duplicator. You can clip these (have you got a stapler handy?) to incoming mail, or simply send them instead of typewritten internal memoranda.

7

MEETINGS

Meetings and committees have a bad reputation as a prime source of annoyance on account of the time wasted. But if they are well planned and run they can be the best (even the only) way to: brief staff on policy, progress, points for action; uncover facts; produce new ideas; get people involved.

The basic skill of the chairperson is in the deft use of questions to stimulate discussion, keeping to the point, summarising, tactfully rejecting irrelevancies, and bringing quiet people in (see Appendix 2).

Participants

To make the best use of the meeting, participants will be:

- knowledgeable of the subject matter; aware of the purpose of the meeting; interested; conscientious (especially about preparing in advance)
- seated in place on time; equipped with the necessary papers and materials
- prepared to air their views strongly, making out a good case; able to keep to the point; ready to listen to other opinions; capable of being reasonably influenced
- disciplined and patient; prepared to contribute their best thinking and experience concisely and at the appropriate times
- reliable in accepting the decision reached and deferring to the control of the chairman, and in carrying out, on schedule, action assigned to them.

They will show skill in:

- producing new ideas
- helping to clarify and develop other people's ideas
- listening
- helping to keep the discussion to the point
- asking for clarification and summaries.

They will not allow emotions, inter-departmental battles or office politics to inject unwanted 'hidden agendas' into the meeting.

8

DELEGATION

Delegation is not 'allocating duties' or 'work scheduling'. It is about letting somebody else do something we would normally do. It demands giving away some of our authority to enforce action. It gives others freedom of action while we continue to carry the can. It is risky and painful. It can seem unnatural to people who have succeeded so far by doing things well themselves.

Example 7
The operations director in an international company was against letting people use their initiative. 'Only after all else has failed.' She had suffered from the results of people dashing about in all directions and going off at half-cock.

Example 8
A city firm reorganised itself into executive and administrative 'committees' after the office manager had overworked himself into an early grave.

There is a clue to the information gap which often occurs somewhere halfway down the organisational pyramid. People get information they are entitled to and proceed to hang on to it, while failing to let their subordinates in on it. The Industrial Society advocates regular briefing by team leaders. Once we find a way to share our knowledge of the common purpose behind all our actions, people can fit their work into the overall picture. This allows them to use their initiative to positive effect. The cycle is illustrated in Fig. 1.

Fig. 1. The team briefing cycle

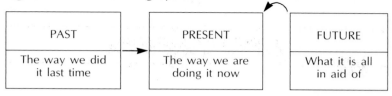

PAST	PRESENT	FUTURE
The way we did it last time	The way we are doing it now	What it is all in aid of

Routine

Most people are working in the 'past', while managers are privileged to be working in the 'future'. Management is involved in defining objectives, conceiving strategy, formulating policy, making plans, setting targets. For the rest, the day is full of routine operations.

This word 'routine' has a mythology of its own. Ask any group of workpeople for their feelings, and they will come up with something like this off-the-cuff answer from a group of computer professionals during an in-house training course:

Work – ugh! – boring (8 people had this) – schedule – task – dull – documentation – terminals.

After five minutes' illustrated talk on how to manage routine, the value of 'drills', they were asked again:

Automated – reducible – useful guidelines – vital – pay somebody else to do it – methods – efficient – necessity – error-reducing – essential – organisation – useful – time-saving – necessary evil – aid – repetitive – with minimum thought.

Why?

There are many good reasons *why* we must delegate:

- to free us to concentrate on more important issues
- to give practical training in the real situation to our staff
- to help people gain self-confidence
- because decisions made closer to the point of action can be taken sooner.

  However, we ought to remind ourselves of the snags.

- Poorer quality of decisions because subordinates lack judgement or expertise. Still, this can be overcome by good selection, training and communication.
- Loss of consistency as more people are involved with decisions. Effective leadership needed.
- Decisions taken by a subordinate lack impact because of absence of authority. So, give them freedom of action, tell others who are involved, and back the person.
- Control is loosened. This is a case for an effective monitoring system.
- It takes longer—in the short term. But the improvement in relationships, coupled with increasing abilities, far outweighs initial disadvantages.
- Danger of confusion between 'responsibility' and 'authority' between the boss and the subordinate. Both need to talk this through. Responsibility is about doing things we have agreed to do; authority is about the right to expect that one's decisions will be carried through.

When?

Next we need to consider *when* to delegate. We can all do it when it is safe and easy, when:

- a decision can be reversed quickly and easily
- the task is repetitive
- the impact on others is slight
- there is low risk of commitment of money and physical resources
- it can be done within existing policies and procedures.

Safe and easy delegation does not encourage involvement or satisfaction. A deliberate effort must be made to unload interesting and challenging tasks (the parts of our job we like, or are good at) and in selecting people with the latent ability. We can build up the necessary evidence for the latter with a properly run performance appraisal system.[4]

How?

As this is a complex process, we must go about it systematically.

1 *Assessment.* Determine (this means 'write down'!) what the task is, what is involved. Decide who is best able to carry it out, or who is most likely to benefit from the opportunity.

2 *Agreement.* You must enter into an arrangement and agree with the person involved exactly:

- what is expected of them
- the time limits
- how the monitoring system is going to operate
- the limits of authority: do they do as they think fit, act and tell you afterwards, or ask before they implement a proposal?

3 *Sustaining.* You must not simply leave them to get on with it, totally unaided. This is known as 'abdication'. Sustain them by:

- giving them the information they need and the tools for the job
- giving them any necessary training
- not breaking the agreement unless absolutely necessary
- providing moral support
- supplying them with immediate knowledge of results as they produce them

- operating the monitoring system on schedule and without oppression.

4 *Accountability.* We know we carry the can. A good way to organise this is to guide the subordinate into 'reporting up' in a form we can use, without editing or embellishing, to keep 'grandfather' informed.

A reminder to avoid:

- over-delegating leading to taking back authority because of excessive delays
- failing to release authority and freedom of action
- giving away the responsibility but taking all the decisions in advance
- giving more freedom of action than subordinates can handle
- breathing down their necks
- direct criticism, putting them on the defensive and demoralising them
- not telling them enough so they have to keep coming back
- failing to be around when they need guidance
- appearing to delegate but in reality only ridding ourselves of things we dislike or expect to be done 'our way'.

Delegation to the worker

Most managers find it easy to give examples of decisions made by their superiors which they feel they should have been allowed to take. Yet the same managers often experience difficulty in drawing up a list of decisions they themselves could have passed down the line. Delegation can only work properly when there is a deliberate and conscious effort to force decisions down to the appropriate level, ideally to the individual who actually does the work.

This last idea comes as a bit of a surprise to managers brought up in the 'old school'. But there is no loss of management control in the factory where steel is bought, not by a highpowered purchasing manager, but by the press operator. The superintendents still 'superintend' in the local authority where the road sweepers get their own brooms instead of arguing with a storekeeper.

9

OTHER PEOPLE'S TIME

Recent studies among middle managers have revealed that they spend about half their time on quite brief contacts, queries, confirmations, and progress chasing. These are unplanned and last from ¾ to 5 minutes. Formal interviews, meetings, correspondence, visits, and telephoning had to be fitted into what remained of the working day. Such impromptu encounters were neither unnecessary, nor useless interruptions, nor trivia. They were essential contacts without which the people on the shop floor would not have been able to get on with their jobs.

Example 9
One personnel manager was avoided as much as possible by her staff because she could not give a quick answer to a quick question. She always wanted to start a conversation.

Example 10
A night shift supervisor in a bakery had a way of taking himself off somewhere out of the way at the first sign of any trouble.

Example 11
A leading group of builders' merchants wanted to install a staff development programme along with an appraisal scheme. At the stage of analysing what the jobs were, some of the managers were astounded at the lack of common perception of what people were actually doing. The overlap between the job description drafted by the architectural ironmongery estimator, and what his manager wrote, amounted to less than 33 per cent (see Fig. 2).

Management sins

Our actions are capable of having a more far reaching effect on those around us than we sometimes admit. Inept delegation can be self-defeating if all we are trying to do is solve our own problems at others' expense.

Are *we* their biggest problem?

In the case of Example 11, the ensuing discussion brought new insight. The office was altered around. A direct line telephone was put on his desk. Much time was saved in staying in touch with manufacturers, architects, site foremen and retail branch managers. He got his own copies of professional journals instead of being 'permitted' to keep those that survived a long circulation list.

Fig. 2. An effect of lack of communication

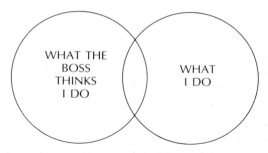

Most of us have been guilty at one time or another of getting in other people's way. As you glance down the following list of 'sins', remember, however, that we have to do some of these things sometimes.

- transmitting information instead of sharing it
- keeping people waiting unnecessarily
- interrupting
- unaccounted-for absence
- destroying people's priorities with continued requests for work

27

- insensitivity to other people's unspoken feelings and ideas
- dropping in for a couple of minutes and wasting the whole afternoon
- forgetting important things, especially passing on informal decisions made over lunch or in the corridor.

Looking and listening

People may not like us cropping up unexpectedly, but they moan if they never see us. The rule when going on our rounds is: have a reason for being there. It is awkward to be cast in the role of visiting VIP, and humiliating to be mistaken for the electrician. Equally, a 'detective' approach will merely generate 'alibis'. Show genuine interest, listen, take notes (put down what *they* want you to remember—you can always make your own notes afterwards). Let them have your reactions, or answers, within 48 hours—even (or perhaps especially) when the answer is 'no'.

Listening has been called the 'lost art of our age'. We have already seen how must faster we can think than the other person can talk. Use the precious seconds. Submerge your own thoughts. Concentrate on what is being said. Show how you are willing to accept their viewpoint, and make an effort to understand. Hold back, wait; open eyes and ears and search for what they mean within what they actually say.

Consideration

When we are trying to uncover facts—at selection, appraisal, grievance or disciplinary interviews—it pays to remember that we can fail by:

- forgetting to remain neutral
- misunderstanding
- jumping to conclusions

- dealing prematurely with situations ('Yes but', 'If I were you', 'I know how you feel', 'What we must do is this')
- rejecting the other person's explanation.

By indulging ourselves in this way we risk evoking fear, hostility, suspicious withdrawal or passive acceptance, which in turn can lead to sullen slavery.

Teamwork

We can waste a lot of time disapproving of other people's attitudes. It is not too helpful to berate young Alec about 'Your attitude, son'. Yet the lad is very willing to adapt what he actually does, minute-by-minute, to co-operate with his supervisor. And it is this the older person should be trying to influence.

A harassed 'team leader' in one of the practical exercises on an Action-Centred Leadership course was listening to the comments of other course members who had been observing her trying to lead four people to complete a task. 'We were only given twenty minutes!' True—if you only count 'elapsed' time. In fact, she had a total of $5 \times 20 = 100$ people/minutes. When this was pointed out, her exasperation disappeared.

People need managers who are expert and friendly: managers who respect their time and aspirations; leaders who can get the best out of all the people/minutes.

10

SECRETARIES

There she sits, mute and resentful. On her last task (over and above typing and filing) she made a mess through being too nervous. No wonder her boss took it over and finished it himself. He still does all his correspondence in longhand and opens all his own mail. Not long to go before five thirty.

The eleventh floor: Henrietta is talking to her visitor about *her* secretary. 'Ideal—does everything for me. Hundred per cent. Finds things I used to lose. Wasn't she tactful about your turning up like this? Better make it brisk, she'll be in in a minute to grab me for that meeting.'

Not two different secretaries: the same one six months later!

Delegation and partnership

Secretaries can tackle many of their boss's tasks on their own. This saves *time* by freeing the boss for other things, and *money*, because their salaries are different. This level of efficiency is not achieved by magic, though some say chemistry comes into it.

Henrietta holds fortnightly 'business meetings' with her secretary. They discuss their work as partners in a joint business. Henrietta realises that there are, in reality, not two jobs but one. The secretary would not be there but for the boss, and the boss could not do her work properly without the secretary's help.

Many managers still expect a brand-new secretary, fresh from the outside world via the personnel department, to plunge straight in. 'Type all right can you?' Time spent at the start of the partnership can save costly mistakes later. Remember the 'past–present–future' model in Chapter 8.

Communication

Many secretaries complain of the silent, disappearing boss who hardly ever speaks except to deliver dictation, and who vanishes without saying where to. Conflict can arise from the differing expectations of boss and secretary. This can be overcome by business meetings coupled with joint target setting[5] along the lines of:

- producing a hand-over list for holiday stand-ins
- listing effect on boss of current legislation
- finding out the sources of power in the firm (other than in the organisation charts)
- compiling a dossier on what the competitors produce.

Working through the following checklist, does your secretary:

- operate her own wall chart showing action planned?
- plan in advance what happens when she is on holiday?
- have a job description, with performance standards, linked to your own?
- say 'we' when referring to you or your work?
- attend meetings with you (and not just to take notes)?
- know what decisions to take, and their implications?
- know how you are getting on?
- know how she is getting on?
- occasionally represent you or the organisation in her own right?
- give her own name when answering the telephone?
- sign her own name (over her own typed name) on routine letters she has written?
- have at least one project, not necessarily secretarial, with full responsibility?
- know the budget, income and expenditure?

Checklist—business meeting agenda

1 Results of any meetings the boss has attended.
2 Future plans affecting the department's work load.
3 Reallocation of priorities so secretary's time can be organised.
4 Checking diaries to see that the same appointments appear in both.
5 Review of telephone calls, action taken and advice for action needed.
6 Potential office problems the boss might not hear about.

The last item ought to help develop trust and confidentiality, and may well help other people to be circumspect in all their dealings with both of you.

11

ROOTS AND BRANCHES

Not many organisations operate entirely under one roof; we are members of teams dispersed throughout the land, and often the world. Some people get lonely, others relish the freedom. The opportunities for wasting time are legion.

Just because an organisation *does* operate within the one site, do not forget that the person two doors along the corridor can feel just as 'left out' as the wandering salesman. There are messages for us all in the experiences recorded in this section.

Example 12
A fast-growing building society recently introduced a policy of centralising systems (their new computer can show every investor's and borrower's account at a touch of the 'send' button) and decentralising decisions—each branch manager has the power to grant mortgages.

Example 13
Three-person teams plan deliveries to new customers from a northern brewery. A salesman and two draymen walk the route, from the proposed parking position right through to the siting of the barrels, and discuss how to do it. It is not often that a delivery to an outlying club or a city-centre steak house is held up because of a last-minute snag.

Example 14
After the monthly briefing meetings of the senior managers in a shipping and forwarding business, each 'top person' climbs into a car and goes out to one of the regions, where the branch managers gather for their briefing. Then the branch managers return to do their meetings locally. The visiting senior manager goes out with a different branch manager in turn.

The multiple retailer stands or falls by the performance of the branch manager.

Example 15

One national chain reports immediately from head office on: the selling price account; the ratio of wages/sales; the branch's league-table position. They leave the local person to handle relations with customers, development, morale of the team, and the expansion of sales. Central specialists give support with buying, processing, book keeping, settlement of prices, point-of-sale display material, and administrative burdens.

Example 16

A leading ethical pharmaceuticals manufacturer sends representatives out to hospitals and general practitioners. Their jovial sales director says he never loses sight of one statistic: 'Young Appleby may only be 1 per cent of our sales force but, to the doctor he sees, he is 100 per cent of our company'.

Much time can be saved in planning journeys. Petrol and shoe leather can be saved if a visitor to an unfamiliar area reads the map intelligently and sequences calls to avoid covering the same ground over and again.

Example 17

A retail regional manager held a meeting with her district managers to discuss journey planning. She put up several maps and charted where several of the district managers had been the previous week. They were all amazed at the level of overlapping and extra miles driven.

Example 18

An area manager got an urgent message while at one branch to visit a branch 20 miles away, immediately. He jumped into his car and drove the 20 miles to find the problem was that one of the strip fluorescent lights had gone and needed to be replaced. The branch didn't have a spare. He sent someone out to buy one and waited until the boy returned so he could put it in!

Checklist

To be covered in discussions with regional/area managers.

- Compiling visit checklists.
- Setting a specific visit objective.
- Having a branch file.
- Organisation of car and briefcase.
- Planning, preparation, priorities.
- Studying the communication at meetings.
- Telling people where you are and can be got hold of.
- Having a base or 'anchor' branch—where all queries and problems are passed to. Some can be answered by the manager of the unit, with proper delegation and training. At least you just have one telephone call to make to find out problems and priorities.
- Spending longer in one location so you can really achieve something, not the twenty-minute 'hello—how are you—goodbye' visit! Spend one, or even two full days.
- Telling managers you're coming, and what you want to talk about, so that they are prepared.
- Analysing the trading pattern and staff coverage.
- Analysing branch layout and equipment; using string diagrams.
- Doing time–task analyses to find out how long things take.
- Managing your own boss!
- Having a written record to ensure follow-up on delegated tasks and points for action.

12

FINDING MORE TIME

Most of us, given the time, would do more of what we are paid to do. We have seen what takes up so much time, seducing us away from what we should be doing. High on the list are the brief contacts, queries and the mundane day-to-day tasks. We get trapped into attempting to control failures when we should be monitoring progress. Too often we are no more than 'visiting firemen'. It would be nice to do the 'coping' at the start instead of trying to cobble it all together at the last moment (see Fig. 3).

Fig. 3. Comparison of unplanned and planned use of time

PUT THE LAST FIRE OUT		PUT THE NEXT FIRE OUT	
PLAN	ORGANISE	MONITOR PROGRESS	ACHIEVE

Elapsed time ⟶

Textbook stuff? Not possible in the real world? Return to page 1 and start again. And do it in the firm's time, too.

Seriously though, instant solutions are not available; offers of a panacea for saving time are mere quackery. But we have to start somewhere, on the little things.

Planning checklist

1 Set long-term objective.
2 Gather facts (opinions, feelings) relevant to the long term.

3   Sort out the facts into various appropriate headings.
4   Figure out the relationships, and the priorities, between the elements.
5   Draw up more than one long-term plan.
6   Try to forecast (this means 'guess'!) the probable outcome of each plan.
7   Select the plan that most closely fits the long-term objective.
8   Set each short-term objective in turn.
9   Gather facts (opinions, feelings) relevant to the short-term.

Long-term can be five years or one week; short-term can be one year or one day.

What to plan for?

There are some things we can't: changes in legislation; breakdowns; delivery failures; industrial trouble in other organisations. These have to be coped with. But we can plan the mundane elements—the routine. We need to rid ourselves of the notion that 'routine' is merely 'boring'. It requires rational redefinition. The first key concept is its repetitive nature. Redefine it as 'regular' or 'recurrent' to take the nasty taste away.

The second key concept is that routine is 'necessary': the trouble here is that the word often goes into the phrase 'necessary *evil*'.

Routines were invented in the first place to ensure success of the total enterprise. For all the statements of objectives, the job descriptions and the checklists, the rule books and manuals of procedure, it is what we *do* that turns the dream into reality. Routines help us, step-by-step, to reach our goal. They are recurrent: they are therefore predictable. So they can be planned.

The common purpose

When each team member is doing his or her bit, that effort added to all the others, combines to take us on our way. It is the common purpose we are all going after that lends dignity to the process. We will know we're getting somewhere when the manager is purely accountable, i.e. when all the *others* in the team are responsible. It is then the manager's privilege to generate the activities of the rest, and to support them in what they are doing.

Time wasters are universal. Devices for saving time tend to be personal. Here are a few collected from life. Pick out and use any that appeal to you.

Example 19
In deciding which receptionists to keep on beyond their initial probationary period, supervisors in an international airline graded individuals by, amongst other factors, what the staff actually did on reporting for duty at the start of a shift. The 'good' ones got in early, took up their positions at the check-in desks, replenished the pigeon-holes with destination labels, filled the stapler, read through the daily list of flights, and the list of expected VIPs. The 'rejects' habitually got in dead on time, were never really ready for the customers and spent the whole 7½ hours in a state of barely controlled fluster, making too many uncorrected mistakes as they went along.

Example 20
An area superintendent for a retail chain was unimpressed to see store managers' desks cluttered with piles of orders, dockets, price lists, and tea-break schedules. Though they might protest that they knew where everything was, he found he could all too frequently catch them out with something important.

Example 21
The optician's assistant who could 'never find anything' was helped by one of the patients — a carpet layer by occupation — who advised her to put things down where they can be seen easily: light things on dark surfaces, dark on light. It pays to notice colour contrasts in the tools of the trade.

Example 22

An office manager refers to the whole of the top surface of her desk as her in-tray. If it is clear, she feels free to patrol other offices, keeping in touch, helping individuals. Each of the drawers, too, has a specific purpose. The top right-hand one she uses as her out-tray. Her secretary, or any of her staff, can—without interrupting her on the telephone, or in a meeting with a visitor—empty this drawer. This is particularly useful when she has some unfinished task in there which someone else can take over while she deals with lengthy interruptions. Papers for the day's meetings, extracted from a brought-forward system, are placed each morning in another drawer reserved for the purpose. There is a drawer to tidy away all the little things: pens and pencils; paperclips; odd foreign stamps. The telephone, and the boss's intercom, are on a side table which has a shelf carrying a dialling code booklet and the manager's 'blue book'. This is a loose-leaf binder with all kinds of items connected with the job and the firm. Plans of how to get there, internal extensions and names, accountability chart, home telephone numbers of key personnel, fire instructions, last year's report and accounts are some of these items.

Example 24

Using a similar concept, a personnel executive at a major computer manufacturing company is able to appear to accomplish many things at once. People peering around his half-open office door can tell at a glance, by whether he keeps his head down or looks up, if they can interrupt him at that instant.

Example 25

An overseas director worked out with her secretary a flexible weekly timetable which is outlined in Fig. 7. Tuesdays and Thursdays were kept for booked appointments and meetings. Monday afternoons, she tended to withdraw to think. Wednesdays she tried to stay in the office doing tasks she didn't mind being taken away from—she was amenable to unplanned interruptions. Friday afternoon was the only time she would sign expense claims. (She wouldn't be drawn about Monday mornings, or Friday mornings for that matter!)

Example 23
An insurance executive imagines large projects as slices of Gruyere cheese, into the 'holes' of which (short periods of waiting time during which he would be held back from the main job) he fits little bits of work.

Figure 4. Example of a weekly timetable

M		Thinking
T	Appointments and meetings	
W	Open door	
Th	Appointments and meetings	
F		'Authority'

II

APPENDICES

APPENDIX 1

TIME SAVERS' CHECKLIST

- Study recurrent crises and find out ways to plan ahead to avoid them.
- Spend more time in future on upward rather than downward communication.
- Think about the boss's problems.
- Keep all your scribbled notes, telephone message slips, and doodles for a period of a month; analyse them and you may find clues to how to save time next month.
- Draw up an occasional 'laundry list' of detailed activities for periods of a half-hour at a time; analyse these and see where the time went.
- Note how long things take.
- Develop a daily/weekly/monthly/annual 'timetable' and encourage others to do the same.
- Learn when to say 'no'.
- Think periodically of what you will do when you retire.
- Get well acquainted with modern mathematical and statistical methods.
- Delegate.
- Ask other people what devices *they* use to save time.
- Schedule active/positive tasks *first*. Build-in interruption allowances and allow time for reactive tasks.
- Avoid lots of short work periods; try to get a continuous stretch.
- Schedule the jobs requiring maximum 'brain capacity' to be carried out when you are at your best.
- Aim to *achieve* something every day.
- Ask yourself regularly: 'What is the best use of my time right now?'

APPENDIX 2

CHAIRING AND LEADING MEETINGS

Meetings are occasions when a group of people come together to share ideas and experiences. They serve a variety of purposes, e.g. information giving, information gathering, persuading, problem solving. The role of the chairman is influenced by that purpose.

Preparation and planning

Consider: purpose, membership, size and agenda.

Arrange: venue (quiet, comfortable, everyone able to see and hear)
visual aids and recording of proceedings.

Plan: procedure, including own introductory statement.

Conducting the meeting

- Create 'climate' by treating members with courtesy, respect and impartiality.
- Open by explaining purpose and procedure.
- Start discussion by an 'overhead' or 'direct' question.
- Encourage full participation: remember that maximum participation by the chairperson means minimum participation by the members.
- Assist communication by asking questions, listening to members' contributions, clarifying misunderstandings, correcting errors, rejecting irrelevancies, co-ordinating ideas, giving information, and summarising.
- Aim for systematic progress towards achieving the purpose of the meeting.
- End meeting by summing up and agreeing conclusions with the group.

Controlling the discussion

Questions
- 'Overhead' question: addressed to group as a whole; engages everyone's attention; avoids putting pressure on individuals before they are ready to answer.
- Direct question: brings in individual with special knowledge, or a reticent member; increases tempo.
- Redirected question: aids continuity; involves other individuals.
- Relay question: readdressing a question, directed at the chairperson to the group for reply.
- Reverse question: get individuals to answer their own questions—polite way of asking them to think again to bring out views they are known to have. (N.B. when addressing a question to individuals, say their name first to engage their full attention.)

Statements
To supply information needed; to stimulate discussion; to clarify or reflect the views of an individual or of the group.

Summaries: interim
Review progress; highlight important points, refocus 'off-track' discussion; change direction; slow down pace of discussion.

Summaries: final
Confirm conclusions; give members a sense of achievement.

Problems

People
- Talkative types: use when relevant and not monopolising conversation—otherwise interrupt, thank for contribution, and redirect question to another member.
- Long-winded types: try and help them express their ideas concisely; be tactful.
- Silent members: encourage and support them—draw them out by asking questions you know they can answer; try to analyse reason for silence.
- The quibblers: want to concentrate on minor points—ask rest of group if they want to do so, or suggest it be deferred.
- Persistent questioners: return questions to them or group if they

are trying to trap chairman; if they genuinely do not understand, try to help them.
- The objectors: can be quarrelsome—ask for their reasons/evidence.
- Dominating types: try to hold back their contribution until others have had their say. (N.B. to counter-balance the above types, encourage the positive members, i.e. knowledgeable, experienced people with a commonsense attitude.)

Situations
- Conflict: hold the ring; relieve tension by rephrasing in less emotive terms, by humour, by change of subject; avoid getting personally involved.
- Unpopular decisions: when under attack from group, continue to argue your case and build on any support from individual members.
- Lack of interest: try to illustrate to group how matter might affect them personally; drop topic temporarily and come back later; change approach.
- Off-the-track or irrelevant questions/discussion: may indicate lack of interest; if genuine concern on a vaguely related issue, try to deal with it quickly; ask relevant question; summarise frequently.
- Confidential information: by accident or design chairperson may be asked for this—state clearly that that information cannot be given, and explain why.

APPENDIX 3

WORKING WITH YOUR SECRETARY— CHECKLIST

Involvement / Time planning

- Ensure secretary understands the responsibilities laid down in your job description.

- Ensure secretary had adequate job description, i.e. activities/ duties relating directly to your key responsibilities (latter indicated on secretary's job description). These first two points will help the secretary recognise the importance of her contribution in achieving results. The dignity of any task is derived directly from the importance of the end result. Also, once one is aware of an objective, freedom to use initiative is given.

- Have a formal, regular planning meeting with your secretary —marked in your diary for the year. Use these meetings to discuss plans, priorities, workloads, etc. If you both keep a checklist of topics to raise at the meeting, these will form the basis of an informal agenda. Avoid unnecessary interruptions during the meetings.

- Encourage secretary to open and *read* all in-coming post, where possible adding relevant background papers and making helpful notations, particularly pointing out action to be taken.

- Allow your secretary to attend department/team meetings where practical. This is an outward sign by you of your confidence. In time, others will begin to use your secretary as your support, e.g. requests for information, appointments, etc., thus releasing your time. The secretary will also be able to help monitor any action arising from such meetings.

- Allow/encourage secretaries to attend any promotion/ conference, etc., for which they have done a great deal of the administration.

- Allow your secretary to control your time—one master diary kept by your secretary and a pocket diary for yourself. When offering times/dates, always say your secretary will confirm. This avoids duplication, allows realistic time-planning, and encourages others to use your secretary.

- Discuss with your secretary ways of time-planning.
  1 *Dictation*—mark in diary regular, lengthy sessions, thus avoiding time-wasting piecemeal dictation.
  2 *Reading*—consider allocating in diary best time for reading, e.g. last half-hour. Maybe preparatory time prior to meetings.
  3 *Report-writing*—can be done in advance for regular reports such as progress, etc.
  4 *Systems*—implementation/development of practical aids and systems often involves a great deal of concentrated secretarial time, e.g. a new filing system. If these are needed, discuss where best they can be fitted into your schedule and give support.

- Encourage drafting of certain correspondence—dictate perhaps only main points. Also allow the writing of routine letters, e.g. confirmation of appointments, over your secretary's own name and title (again, a projection of confidence/efficiency) which reflects back on you and your section/department.

APPENDIX 4

REFERENCES

1   Grummitt, J. *Rapid reading*. Communication Skills Guide. London: The Industrial Society, 1987.
2   Vidal-Hall, J. *Report writing*. Communication Skills Guide. London: The Industrial Society, 1988.
3   Devery, C. *Working with management: a secretary's guide*. London: The Industrial Society, 1987.
4   Lawson, I. *Appraisal and appraisal interviewing*. Notes for Managers series. London: The Industrial Society, 1989.
5   Lawson, I. *Target setting*. Notes for Managers series. London: The Industrial Society, 1989.

FURTHER READING

Adair, J. *How to manage your time*. Guildford: The Talbot Adair Press, 1987.

Adair, J. *The effective communicator*. London: The Industrial Society/Kogan Page, 1988.

Devery, C. *Working with a secretary: a manager's guide*. London: The Industrial Society, 1986.

Forrest, A. *Delegation*. Notes for Managers series. London: The Industrial Society, 1989.

Garnett, J. *The manager's responsibility for communication*. Notes for Managers series. London: The Industrial Society, 1989.

Pemberton, M. *Effective meetings*. Communications Skills Guide. London: The Industrial Society, 1988.